T0157499

Conscious
PARENTING

NURTURING THE CONNECTION

REGINA FRIDKIN

"Practicing mindful parenting while fostering
the growth of children's talents and providing
an environment for them to flourish."

BALBOA.PRESS
A DIVISION OF HAY HOUSE

Balboa Press books may be ordered through booksellers or by contacting:

Balboa Press
A Division of Hay House
1663 Liberty Drive
Bloomington, IN 47403
www.balboapress.com
844-682-1282

Because of the dynamic nature of the Internet, any web addresses or
links contained in this book may have changed since publication and
may no longer be valid. The views expressed in this work are solely those
of the author and do not necessarily reflect the views of the publisher,
and the publisher hereby disclaims any responsibility for them.

The author of this book does not dispense medical advice or prescribe the use
of any technique as a form of treatment for physical, emotional, or medical
problems without the advice of a physician, either directly or indirectly. The
intent of the author is only to offer information of a general nature to help
you in your quest for emotional and spiritual well-being. In the event you use
any of the information in this book for yourself, which is your constitutional
right, the author and the publisher assume no responsibility for your actions.

Any people depicted in stock imagery provided by Getty Images are
models, and such images are being used for illustrative purposes only.
Certain stock imagery © Getty Images.

Print information available on the last page.

ISBN: 979-8-7652-4863-8 (sc)
ISBN: 979-8-7652-4864-5 (e)

Balboa Press rev. date: 02/14/2024

CONTENTS

NURTURING THE CONNECTION

In the early stages of parenthood, we begin to establish an understanding and connection with our child. It is critical to have clear intentions as a parent in this stage. When your child is brought into this world, it is your responsibility, as a parent, to provide the bare necessities for their survival. However, despite all you may provide for your child, they will not truly thrive without love. To nurture the connection with your child, you must employ intention, attention, awareness, and love.

The intention forms the relationship's foundation, steering interactions, and choices. Attention demands active involvement in the child's life, acknowledging their unique needs, interests, and emotions. Awareness requires understanding the child's developmental phases and adapting parenting strategies to meet these evolving needs. Love, essential for a secure and nurturing environment, provides constant support and heartfelt affection. Love instills a sense of worth and belonging, crucial for emotional and psychological development.

Nurturing the connection is a dynamic and ongoing journey. It calls for patience, flexibility, and a readiness to grow together with your child.

PREFACE

A JOURNEY OF CONSCIOUS PARENTING

This book is dedicated to my beautiful two daughters, my pride and joy. They have been the driving force behind my inspiration to write about conscious parenting. From the depths of my heart, I want to provide them with a nurturing and thriving environment, not only for their growth but also for the growth of everyone I come in contact with.

Ever since I was a little girl, my greatest dream was to become a mother. I longed to embrace the role of a caregiver and to witness the miracle of life unfolding before my eyes. But the path to motherhood was not immediate. It took time and patience for me to find my soulmate, a partner who would not only be an incredible father but also share my vision of conscientious parenting.

Conscious parenting is an approach to parenting that involves being mindful, present, and intentional in the way parents interact with their children. It emphasizes cultivating a deep understanding of oneself and one's child, fostering a strong parent-child connection, and making conscious choices in parenting practices.

Today, as I write these words, I am happily married to my soulmate for almost twenty years. Our journey together has been filled with love, growth, and countless lessons. Raising our two amazing daughters has been an incredible blessing, and I am profoundly grateful for this gift.

Throughout the years, I have encountered numerous individuals—friends, teachers, colleagues—who have marveled at the character and qualities of my children. They often approached me, seeking insights into the secret behind raising such remarkable kids. It was during these moments that I realized my experiences could be valuable to others on their own parenting journeys.

I began to jot down notes, capturing the essence of my approach to conscious parenting. These scribbles and reflections served as a testament to my dedication, as I am eager to share my insights with the world. Today, when my oldest has graduated high school with honors and begun her journey to university, and my youngest has entered her junior year in high school, inspired me to reflect on those notes and an embodiment of my experiences, wisdom, and heartfelt intentions and share them with you.

In the pages that follow, I invite you to join me on a journey of conscious parenting. Through these words, I hope to inspire and guide you as you connect with your own children. This is not a manual or a set of rigid rules but a source of inspiration, a guiding light, to help you create meaningful connections and foster an environment of love and growth.

May the stories and lessons shared here resonate with you, reminding you of the infinite potential that lies within both you and your child. Together, let us embark on this beautiful expedition on conscious parenting as we nurture not only our children but also ourselves along the way.

With love and gratitude,
Regina

Chapter 1

UNLEASHING POTENTIAL: NURTURING CONFIDENCE, EMPOWERING TALENTS, AND CULTIVATING LEADERSHIP

Through nurturing my kids' unique talents, embracing their self-perceptions, and fostering leadership skills, I have witnessed the profound impact of conscious parenting on their lives. Conscious parenting is a mindful and compassionate way of raising children. It involves being aware and attentive to our own emotions and actions as well as to our children's needs and feelings. It focuses on building a strong bond between parent and child and making thoughtful decisions about how we parent.

EMBRACING PASSION AND IDENTITY

When my daughter, at the age of seven, confidently declared herself a violinist, I initially dismissed her claim, stating, "No, you are not. You are just learning how to play." However, her unwavering belief and determination challenged my perspective. Realizing the power of my words, I chose to embrace her identity as violinist. At that moment, I understood that maybe I should just step aside and let her have fun. Through support, encouragement, and validation, her love for the violin flourished. This experience taught me the importance of acknowledging and nurturing our children's passions, embracing their self-perceptions, and creating an environment where they can develop confidence and authenticity. She got her violin lessons, practiced with passion, and both my husband and I supported her with smiles. To this day, she plays. It's a way for her to express her emotions and experience joy. I am scared to imagine that I could have prevented that if I went with my initial response of convincing her that she was not.

PAVING THE WAY FOR TALENTS TO FLOURISH

Simultaneously, I encountered the unique challenge of nurturing my youngest daughter's remarkable giftedness. She displayed an exceptional talent for just about anything she set her mind to. As her mom, my role was to pave the way for her, creating opportunities for her to explore and develop her talents. By providing diverse experiences, resources, and freedom of choice, I supported both of my kids in discovering their interests and embracing their own path.

I learned that parenting requires a delicate balance between supporting and nurturing our children's talents while allowing them the freedom to explore and make their own choices. In addition to their talents, both of my daughters demonstrated remarkable leadership skills and a strong commitment to volunteer and involvement in their school as well as community. I recognized the importance of nurturing their leadership qualities through guidance, mentorship, and opportunities for growth. The experiences I had with my children taught me that parenting involves nurturing empathy, compassion, and a sense of social responsibility in them.

Imagine your daughter, a motivated middle school student, takes on a leadership role in the student government and spearheads an initiative to install stop signs in the community for enhanced safety. As a supportive parent, you empower her by providing information about available resources and guiding her in using them effectively. With determination and independent decision-making, she conducts research, gathers data, and presents a compelling proposal to the relevant authorities. Through her own efforts and resourcefulness, she successfully navigates the process and the community begins to see the positive impact of her leadership. This experience not only creates a sense of responsibility and initiative but also reinforces belief in her ability to make a tangible difference through her own actions.

Guiding our children and teaching them how to work independently requires teaching them to think for themselves. When my girls were in kindergarten, they had a lot of homework that often required parental guidance. I noticed that some moms went overboard and ended up doing the projects for their kids. As a result, even in middle school, their children still needed assistance with their work.

My approach was to teach, demonstrate, and encourage my girls to do things themselves, even if it didn't look perfect in my eyes. I had to step back and let their creativity flourish. Until about second grade, I would sit next to my children and watch them complete their homework, providing guidance and assistance when needed. By the time they reached third grade, my girls had become more independent. While I still checked their homework once it was done, I refrained from hovering over them to get it finished.

After completing their work, they were rewarded with engaging activities. Sometimes we even incorporated the homework lessons into play, using them as examples. This approach helped make learning enjoyable and allowed them to see the practical application of their schoolwork in daily life.

By adopting this strategy, I aimed to strike a balance between guidance and independence. I provided my children with the necessary tools and support, while also giving them the freedom to explore and learn on their own. This approach prepared them for future challenges and facilitated their personal growth.

Investing in our children doesn't have to be expensive or solely about material possessions. The true value lies in spending quality time with them and being present in their lives. When we prioritize their needs and interests, we create meaningful connections that are incredibly fulfilling for both parents and children.

By engaging in activities together, we create lasting memories and strengthen the parent-child bond. It's not about the cost or extravagance of the activity but the shared experiences and the joy of being present in those moments. Whether it's playing a game, taking a walk, or having heart-to-heart conversations, these moments of connection provide immense value and nourish the parent-child relationship.

When we invest our time and emotional presence, we gain a deeper understanding of our children. We learn about their passions, strengths, and challenges. This understanding allows us to offer the support and guidance they need to thrive. By being present, we show our children that they are loved, heard, and valued.

Moreover, spending quality time with our children benefits us as parents as well. It brings us joy, fulfillment, and a sense of purpose. Sharing laughter, experiences, and meaningful conversations with our children creates precious memories that we will cherish for a lifetime.

In essence, investing in our children is not about material wealth or extravagant activities. It's about prioritizing their wellbeing, spending quality time together, and nurturing the parent-child relationship. When we invest in their emotional and social development, we provide them with the foundation to grow into confident, happy individuals. The returns on this investment are immeasurable and enrich both our lives and the lives of our children.

The journey of parenting has been a transformative one shaping not only the lives of my daughters but also my own perspective as a parent. Through embracing their passions, empowering their talents, and fostering leadership qualities, I have witnessed their remarkable growth, confidence, and fulfillment. My desire to share the principles and experiences guided me on this journey.

My way of parenting was inspired by recognizing the importance of self-realization and the ability to experience life in the present moment. I believe that life is too short to live someone else's dreams and that we are here to experience life and our human experience fully. As parents, we have the incredible opportunity to connect with our children and learn from their natural talents and wisdom, which can remind us of our purpose in life.

Through parenting with awareness, we can create a more harmonious and fulfilling family dynamic whereby parents and children work together to achieve common goals. By being present in the moment, we can better understand our children's needs, interests, and unique personalities. This allows us to create a more supportive and nurturing environment where our children can thrive and develop to their fullest potential.

Whether you are a new parent navigating the early stages of parenthood or have been raising children for years, every moment presents an opportunity for insightful parenting. Imagine this: You're strolling in a park with your child hand in hand and notice a beautiful flower blooming. Instead of hurrying past, you pause together to appreciate its vibrant colors and delicate petals. In that shared moment, you teach your child the art of mindfulness, guiding them to notice and embrace the beauty in the present moment. As their eyes light up with wonder, you realize that by being fully present, you inspire not only your child but also yourself to live with joy and fulfillment. This simple act of pausing and connecting with the world around you becomes a powerful lesson reminding you to slow down, savor the present, and find beauty in the smallest of moments.

Chapter 2

UNRAVELING THE ESSENCE

How do you live your purpose? How many times were you told what to do? How to act? Where to live, what to wear, what to eat, and so on, constantly chasing the image presented to you by our society and dictated by others?

What is the purpose? What are we trying to prove? Who are we chasing and letting us convince us of what matters most?

Stop and smell the roses, or better yet, just stop and breathe for a minute and realize that life is a gift that is sometimes taken for granted.

From the day that we are born, we take on genetic memory of our parents, grandparents, as well as our environment that molds us into the people we become. How do you live your true purpose and not what is being forced at you? When all of your life you were thought to learn to seek to question and to search outside yourself. As you are born into this remarkable and unknown world and take your first breath, you are in the state of wonder of what is next. It's funny how most of us, when we are all grown up, don't even think about what we were thinking back then. Memories of childhood are very limited to certain milestones that are reminded to us through family, pictures, and stories that are shared with us and retold though out our lifetime.

Do what feels good! When we were children, we were told to not do this or that and that we needed to behave properly, eat a certain way, walk a certain way, and talk in the way that was acceptable by those who were around us. How about discovering your own way? Our personality is mostly created by the environment that we are exposed to at the time of our growth. If our parents are having issues in communication with one another or people in their circle, we absorb that and mold ourselves to what works for us. This is the time when we form beliefs that later power us or limit us. If you look at the innocence of a child, there are no restrictions of pure love and joy. Why does it eventually fade out and then take a lifetime to be found again? When you are a baby, you are enough! Nothing else is expected from you other than that you are a happy baby. And then after a certain age, usually the age when you are off to school, life transitions into expectation of outside conditioning to you being happy and those around you seeing you happy only if those conditions are met.

In a world where we often feel lost and disconnected from our true selves, this book serves as a guide to help readers tap into their inner power and awaken their true potential.

As a parent, one of the most important things we want for our children is for them to lead fulfilling and meaningful lives. We want them to look back on their lives with a sense of satisfaction, knowing that they made a positive impact on the world and lived in alignment with their values. But how do we help our children find their true purpose in life? And how do we ensure they don't look back on their lives with regrets? In this book, I want to share with you some advice and guidance to help your kids live with no regrets.

I remember when I was a young adult trying to figure out what I wanted to do with my life. My personal growth journey has been marked by significant transitions and changes, each leading me down a path of fulfillment and purpose. As a young immigrant teen and a first-generation college graduate in United States, I was guided by my parents, teachers, and professors to get a degree and profession that would give me stability and a paycheck. I loved arts and design yet I ended up in the business management and finance, which led me to find myself immersed in the corporate finance industry working hard to climb the ladder and achieve success. Nevertheless every time I achieved a raise or promotion, I was not satisfied; something was always missing. So I jumped from one company to another never having an issue with finding a job; somehow it always found me.

However, my priorities shifted when I became a parent and decided to leave my career to focus on raising my children. This transition was exciting to me, and to this day, I am beyond grateful to my husband for providing the opportunity to take time off for me for the first few years to be a stay-at-home mom with my kids. I had to learn new skills, balancing the responsibilities of running a household and being present for my children.

Even though I worked for over ten years in the corporate world, I was still looked down upon for being a stay-at-home mom. Becoming a parent was absolutely the most amazing thing in my life. When my girls went to school, I returned to work to make sure that my husband and I can provide the best for our family. Despite the challenges of being a property manager in high-rise condominiums on call twenty-four/seven, parenthood, and caring for my parents whom I lost to cancer, I always kept it together without questioning my purpose.

As I look back, I remember that I was always aligned with my values. Family, kids, and unconditional love were and still some of my top values. Over time, I felt called to pursue a new career path as a life coach and energy healer whereby I could help others find their own paths to fulfillment and happiness. I wanted to inspire people to be their authentic selves and embrace their unique journeys.

As a coach and healer, I strive to convey key messages to my clients, including the importance of self-discovery, self-care, and self-love. I help them uncover their true selves and find the courage to pursue their passions, even if it means stepping outside their comfort zones.

Through my personal growth journey, I have learned that embracing change can lead to incredible opportunities for growth and fulfillment. By following my heart and embracing new paths, I have found joy and purpose in my life, and I hope to inspire others to do the same. Since I had been a little girl, I had dreamed of being a mother—someone who gives life and nurtures the gifts and talents of her children. Now as a proud mom of two amazing kids, I have dedicated my life to helping them be authentic and happy individuals. My mission is to convey the message that *you are enough* and that every person has what it takes to create a fulfilling life.

I have been asked many times about my secret for getting my kids and those around me to accomplish tasks. Why is it so difficult for some parents to get their kids to do what is expected of them? I believe that when we force our expectations and dreams onto our children (or anyone else for that matter) and the outcome doesn't meet our expectations, we become disappointed and discouraged. We create problems by projecting ourselves onto our kids and forcing them to be what we think they should be according to external influences and expectations. Instead, I believe that every person, including every child, is amazing. When we honor who we are and stay true to ourselves, our lives become abundant and exciting. Every human being has the opportunity to experience life, and by honoring and accepting oneself, one can create a life of infinite possibilities for oneself and others.

As a child, I couldn't wait to grow up, but from an early age, I was expected to behave a certain way and do well in school. I'm grateful to my mother for taking the time to show me the beauty of the world—to appreciate nature, smell the flowers, feel the wind, and listen to beautiful music. She also taught me to respect my elders and listen to what they had to say. I'll always remember her words. "It's important to hear what people are saying, but remember to do what you think is right for you." It was great advice, but it took me a while to fully understand and apply it.

The development of a child is deeply influenced by the interplay of genetic memory inherited from parents and grandparents, as well as by the surrounding environment. While parents often harbor aspirations for their children, aiming for prestigious professions like doctors or lawyers, this sometimes reflects more about societal expectations than the child's personal interests and abilities. A trend of competitive parenting has also emerged, where parents vie to present their children as excelling in various fields, whether in arts, sports, or academics, often creating unrealistic standards. However, there's a growing shift towards recognizing the unique talents of each child, understanding that every individual possesses distinct abilities and strengths. This new perspective emphasizes the interconnectedness of individuals and their environments, highlighting the importance of nurturing a child's individuality rather than conforming to societal norms. Parents play a crucial role in this process, not just by guiding their children but also by being role models themselves. It's essential for parents to embody the values and behaviors they wish to instill in their children, thereby creating an environment where children can grow into their best selves, uninhibited by external pressures and expectations.

Chapter 3

EMBRACING SOUL CONTRACTS

In the ethereal realms of existence, where time is but a shimmering illusion, our souls embark on a sacred journey before descending into the embrace of earthly life. In this realm of infinite possibilities, our souls, imbued with ancient wisdom, carefully choose the parents and families that will become the canvas for our soul's growth and evolution. These soul contracts, woven with the threads of love and learning, manifest as the profound bond between parents and children, a reflection of the grand dance of souls.

Conscious parenting is a spiritual voyage that encourages us to embrace the notion that our children are not chance occurrences in our lives. Instead, they are divine manifestations of love and learning, carefully selected to facilitate our soul's exploration of life's sacred mysteries.

Imagine a child whose heart exudes an exceptional sense of compassion and empathy for all living beings. It is likely that this radiant soul has chosen parents who possess the seeds of compassion within their own hearts, though these seeds may yearn for nurturing and awakening. In this sacred contract, the child serves as a guiding light gently leading the parents to explore the depths of their compassion and rediscover the profound interconnectedness that unites all beings. The child's presence becomes a conduit for the parents' journey toward embracing the inherent oneness of all existence.

Similarly, our children may emerge into this world with an innate passion for creativity, expansion into the realms of art, music, or storytelling with unbridled enthusiasm. Their souls might have chosen parents who possess artistic potential yet may have stifled their own creative expressions due to societal conditioning or self-doubt. The child's artistic spirit serves as a catalyst inspiring the parents to break free from the shackles of inhibition and express their unique creative gifts to the world. Together, parent and child embark on a harmonious symphony of creation and self-discovery.

At times, challenges and conflicts may arise within the parent-child relationship, seemingly testing the very essence of our souls. A child struggling with feelings of inadequacy or anxiety may have chosen parents who carry unresolved emotional wounds from their past. In this profound contract, the child acts as a mirror, reflecting the parents' inner journey toward healing and self-acceptance. The transformative power of love and understanding guides both parent and child on a path of healing, culminating in the transcendence of ancestral patterns and the awakening of their divine essence.

Conscious parenting also invites us to embrace the idea that soul contracts are not merely shaped by harmonious choices. Souls may deliberately choose to undergo profound challenges and lessons through their parent-child connection, leading to seemingly paradoxical situations where good children may find themselves facing difficult parents, and vice versa.

For instance, a gentle and compassionate soul, overflowing with love and kindness, might embark on a journey with parents who struggle with anger or emotional turmoil. In this complex dynamic, the child's soul chooses to serve as a beacon of light emanating unconditional love and understanding to help their parents navigate their own emotional landscapes. Their presence becomes a catalyst for the parents to confront and heal their inner wounds, ultimately leading to spiritual growth and transformation.

Conversely, a child who is grappling with their own internal challenges, such as anger or rebelliousness, may align with parents who are exceptionally patient, compassionate, and understanding. In this profound arrangement, the child's soul seeks the support and guidance necessary to overcome their inner struggles. The parents in turn evolve through the unconditional love and acceptance they offer, learning valuable lessons in empathy and nonjudgment.

In the big picture of life, the souls of parents and children are brought together by a profound interconnectedness that transcends traditional concepts of fairness and punishment. The complexity of the universe weaves together souls with different paths and challenges as they interlace their destinies to support each other's growth.

Conscious parenting urges us to embrace this higher perspective, transcending judgment and comparisons. Instead, we learn to celebrate the uniqueness of each soul's journey, understanding that the challenges faced by our children and ourselves are stepping stones toward greater self-awareness and spiritual evolution. Through compassion, acceptance, and a deep understanding of the soul's purpose, we nurture an environment where love becomes the catalyst for profound transformation.

As we walk this path of parenting, we honor the dance of mirrored reflections between parent and child. We cherish the beauty and intricacy of our soul contracts, recognizing the profound wisdom and love that underlie each connection. In this sacred embrace, we learn to cocreate an environment of growth and unconditional love whereby parent and child journey together, intertwined in the eternal tapestry of existence.

Chapter 4

INSPIRING GREATNESS

Encouraging children to take action in life is crucial to their growth and development. Here are some guidelines to inspire kids to be more proactive and engaged in the world around them, instead of being glued to video games:

1. Be a role model. Children tend to imitate their parents' behavior. Thus, it's important to lead by example and demonstrate an active and engaged lifestyle. Encourage outdoor activities, volunteer work, and other social activities that involve interaction with people.
2. Set goals. Help your child set realistic goals and objectives. Break bigger goals into smaller, more achievable steps. Celebrate their successes along the way to keep them motivated.
3. Foster independence. Give your child the freedom to make choices and decisions. Empower them to take responsibility for their own life. This can help develop a sense of ownership and accountability.
4. Limit screen time. While it's OK to indulge in video games and other forms of screen entertainment, it's important

to set limits. Encourage your child to engage in a variety of activities, including physical exercise, socializing, and creative pursuits.

5. Encourage socialization. Children need social interaction to develop communication skills and build relationships. Encourage your child to participate in group activities, clubs, and organizations that align with their interests.

6. Help them find their passion. Encourage your child to explore different interests and activities to find what they enjoy doing. Once they find their passion, support and nurture it to help them develop their skills.

7. Promote empathy and kindness. Encourage your child to be empathetic toward others and to show kindness in their interactions. This can help them develop strong relationships and a sense of community.

In today's fast-paced and technology-driven world, it can be easy for parents to assume that their children are being adequately parented by the school or the community. However, this assumption can lead to a significant disconnect between parents and their children, ultimately hindering the child's personal and academic growth. It is crucial for parents to be actively involved in their child's life. Ask about their experiences, and listen to them.

Parental involvement is essential for a child's personal, academic, and social success. By understanding the impact of parental involvement, communicating effectively with children, being present and involved in their lives, and overcoming barriers to parental involvement, parents can positively influence their children's development and success. It is important for parents to recognize that they are the primary caregivers and role models for their children and should not assume that school or the community will parent their kids. The reason why there is often a disconnect in families is due to a lack of communication and involvement.

Chapter 5

MASTERING THE ART OF EFFECTIVE COMMUNICATION

HOW TO COMMUNICATE EFFECTIVELY WITH CHILDREN

Get down to their level. For example, if you're talking to a young child about their day at school, squat down to their height and maintain eye contact. It shows them that you value their perspective and are actively listening.

1. Use age-appropriate language. For example, instead of saying, "I'm incredibly fatigued," you can say, "I'm very tired." This way, you are using language that the child can understand without overwhelming them with complex words.

2. Listen actively.
   When a child tells you about their drawing, listen attentively, ask follow-up questions, and respond with genuine interest. This encourages them to share more and helps them feel valued.

3. Avoid criticizing or belittling.

   Instead of saying, "You didn't do a good job on your project," try saying, "You put a lot of effort into this project. Next time, let's work on a few areas to make it even better." This approach acknowledges their effort while providing constructive feedback.

4. Show empathy.

   If a child is upset because they lost a game, you can say, "I can see you're feeling disappointed. It's tough to lose, but remember it's about having fun and learning from the experience."

5. Use positive body language.

   Smile when a child tells a joke or shares an exciting story. Maintain eye contact and nod along to show that you're engaged and interested in what they're saying.

6. Use humor.

   If a child is feeling nervous about starting a new school, you can say, "Don't worry. The teachers are friendly, and you'll have so many new friends that your lunchbox won't fit all the snacks!"

7. Set boundaries.

   Let the child know that it's not acceptable to interrupt a conversation, and explain that you will give them your undivided attention as soon as you finish speaking to someone else.

8. Be patient.

   If a child is struggling to express themselves, give them time to gather their thoughts. Avoid rushing them or finishing their sentences. Let them know that you're there to listen and will wait for them to share when they're ready.

9. Be respectful.
   When a child expresses their opinion, even if it differs from yours, acknowledge their perspective and say, "That's an interesting point. I appreciate your thoughts on this matter."

Remember these examples can be adjusted based on the age and developmental stage of the child you are communicating with.

HOW TO COMMUNICATE EFFECTIVELY WITH TEENS

1. Get down to their level.
   When discussing a topic with a teenager, sit next to them or maintain an eye-level conversation. It conveys that you respect their growing independence and see them as equals.

2. Use age-appropriate language.
   Instead of saying, "I'm going to the grocery store to procure some provisions," you can say, "I'm going to the store to get some groceries." Using language that aligns with their everyday vocabulary helps foster understanding.

3. Listen actively.
   When a teenager shares their thoughts or experiences, provide your undivided attention, avoid interrupting, and respond with empathy and understanding. Encourage them to express themselves freely.

4. Avoid criticizing or belittling.

   Instead of saying, "You never take anything seriously," try saying, "I noticed that sometimes you approach things with a more relaxed attitude. Can you tell me why that is?" This approach encourages open dialogue without sounding judgmental.

5. Show empathy.

   If a teenager expresses frustration about a challenging assignment, you can say, "I understand that this assignment is overwhelming for you. Is there anything specific I can do to support you?"

6. Use positive body language.

   Maintain an open and relaxed posture, make occasional eye contact, and nod in agreement or understanding when a teenager is sharing their thoughts or concerns. It shows that you value their perspective.

7. Use humor.

   If a teenager is feeling stressed about an upcoming exam, you can say, "Remember the exam is just a piece of paper trying to make you nervous. You've got this!"

8. Set boundaries.

   Establish clear guidelines about curfew, screen time, or household chores, and explain the reasoning behind them. Encourage open discussion if they have concerns or suggestions.

9. Be patient.

   If a teenager is hesitant to discuss a sensitive issue, give them space and time. Assure them that you're available whenever they're ready to talk, and emphasize that you're there to support them.

10. Be respectful.
    When a teenager shares their opinion on a current event, even if it differs from your own, respond with respect and say, "I appreciate hearing your perspective. It's interesting to consider different viewpoints."

Remember every teenager is unique, and understanding their individual needs and preferences is essential for effective communication. Adapt these examples to suit the specific situation and the teenager's personality and interests.

How to Communicate with Adult Children

Effective communication with adult children is key to maintaining strong relationships and fostering understanding. Firstly, it is important to listen actively, showing genuine interest in their thoughts and feelings. Take the time to hear them out without interrupting or passing judgment. Acknowledge their perspectives and validate their emotions, even if you may disagree.

Secondly, be mindful of your own communication style and tone. Speak respectfully and avoid being overly critical or controlling. Use "I" statements to express your own feelings and experiences, promoting open dialogue instead of defensiveness. Additionally, establish clear boundaries and expectations while allowing for their independence and autonomy. Treat them as equals, recognizing their adult status and respecting their choices.

Lastly, make an effort to keep the lines of communication open, whether through regular phone calls, visits, or digital means. Show interest in their lives, ask open-ended questions, and share your own experiences to foster a sense of connection. By practicing these principles, you can create a foundation of effective communication and strengthen your relationship with your adult children. Also remember that actions speak louder than words.

Chapter 6

THE QUEST FOR PURPOSE

WHAT IS THE TRUE PURPOSE IN LIFE?

It's a question that has perplexed philosophers, theologians, and everyday people for centuries. Some might say it is achieving wealth and success, while others might say it's about finding happiness and inner peace. But for me, true purpose in life is about living in alignment with your values, using your unique talents and skills to make a positive impact on the world, and finding joy and fulfillment in the process.

Adults are often seen as being wiser due to their age and life experience. However, this is not always the case. We should keep in mind that we are all temporary visitors on this earth, here to learn and experience life as humans. As we grow older, we may become more aware of the things we don't know and the areas in which we still need to grow and learn.

One such area where we may need to adapt and learn is in the realm of parenting. Many traditional protocols for controlling children are no longer effective with the new generation. In the past, parents may have relied on strict discipline and punishment to teach their children right from wrong. However, today's children often respond better to a more flexible and empathetic approach. For example, constantly telling a child what to do and how to behave may create a power struggle and lead to rebellion. Instead, parents may find that discussing and negotiating with their child can lead to more positive results.

It is important for parents to recognize that every child is unique and requires a customized approach to parenting. What worked for one child in the past may not work for another child today. Rather than imposing outdated methods and protocols on their children, parents should aim to understand their child's personality, temperament, and individual needs. By doing so, parents can adjust their parenting style to suit the specific needs of their child.

Ultimately, the privilege of becoming a parent is an opportunity to observe and experience the beautiful development of a unique human being. As parents, we should aim to guide and nurture our children's growth in a way that encourages independence, critical thinking, and self-discovery. By embracing this approach, we can create a more positive and fulfilling parenting experience for both us and our children.

The following are some key concepts related to finding true purpose in life:

- **Living in alignment with your values**
  When you live in alignment with your values, you are living in a way that feels authentic and true to who you are. This can help you find a sense of purpose and meaning in life.

  Values are essential aspects of our lives that shape who we are and what we believe in. Recognizing your core values is an important step in understanding your priorities and making decisions that align with what is most important to you. To recognize your values, you can start by reflecting on what matters most to you and what you believe in. Think about your experiences, your role models, and the people or things that inspire you. Pay attention to how you behave in different situations and what motivates you. Your values can also be revealed through your emotions, such as when you feel proud, happy, or fulfilled. Once you have identified your core values, you can use them to guide your decisions and actions and ensure that you are living a life that is true to yourself.

- **Using your unique talents and skills**
  We all have unique talents and skills that we can use to make a positive impact on the world. By using these talents, we can find fulfillment and purpose in our work and our lives.

  Your superpower is the unique combination of talents, skills, and strengths that sets you apart from others and enables you to make a positive impact on the world.

- **Finding joy and fulfillment**
  When we pursue our true purpose in life, we are more likely to find joy and fulfillment in what we do. This can lead to a sense of satisfaction and contentment that lasts a lifetime.

Chapter 7

DISCOVERING AND HARNESSING YOUR SUPERPOWER

Identifying your superpower can take some time and introspection. The following are questions to help you get started:

- What do you enjoy doing in your spare time?
- What are you naturally good at?
- What are some skills you've developed over time?
- What makes you feel energized and fulfilled?
- What do others often come to you for help or advice with?

By reflecting on these questions, you can begin to identify your superpower and gain a deeper understanding of what makes you unique.

DEVELOPING YOUR SUPERPOWER

Once you've identified your superpower, it's important to continue developing it. This can be done through practice, education, and seeking new experiences. Here are some ways to develop your superpower:

1. Practice regularly.
    Whether it's writing, public speaking, or playing an instrument, practice is key to developing your superpower.

2. Seek education and training.
    Taking classes or attending workshops can help you develop your skills and gain new knowledge.

3. Learn from others.
    Seek out mentors or role models who have similar superpowers and learn from their experiences.

4. Try new things.
    Exploring new hobbies or activities can help you discover new talents and develop new skills.

Chapter 8

AWARENESS IN ACTION

I want to talk to you about something very important: self-awareness and recognizing and nurturing your unique talents and abilities. It's essential to understand who you are and what you want in life so you can set goals and take action toward achieving them.

Many people tend to go on autopilot, blocking their feelings and not even realizing that they're not sure what their goals are. Self-awareness is at the very center of your core, and it's the first step toward understanding what you want out of life.

One way to develop self-awareness is by practicing gratitude. Take a moment each day to be grateful for all the good things in your life. Being grateful helps you appreciate what you already have and start the process of understanding your basic needs and desires.

Meditation is another powerful tool for self-awareness. When you quiet your mind and tune out the noise of the outside world, you can hear yourself more clearly. You can identify your values and beliefs and gain a deeper understanding of what you want out of life.

Once you have a clear sense of your desires and goals, it's important to take action toward achieving them. Exploring your options and taking small steps can help you make progress and ultimately get the results you want.

But it's not always easy to take action. Sometimes, we block our feelings and get caught up in the day-to-day demands of life. We forget to listen to ourselves and make choices that align with our true desires.

To get to that alignment, you must remember not to fear your emotions. Your emotions are a guide to where you are and where you want to be. Listen to them and use them to guide your choices. If something doesn't feel right, it probably isn't.

It's important to take responsibility for your choices and actions. Blaming others for your mistakes or shortcomings won't help you grow or achieve your goals. You must accept responsibility and take ownership of your life.

As you embark on your journey toward self-awareness and goal setting, remember that everyone has unique talents and abilities. It's important to recognize and nurture these talents and to allow them to flourish.

Parents, guardians, and mentors play a crucial role in shaping and guiding the development of a child's talents. Recognize and value individual differences and provide a positive and supportive environment for growth and development.

For example, if you notice that your child has a talent for music, provide them with access to musical instruments, lessons, and opportunities to perform. If they have a talent for writing, give them books and writing materials and encourage them to express their ideas and thoughts.

Remember each person has their own unique set of skills and strengths. It's not fair to judge or compare them to others who have different abilities. Encourage your children to pursue their interests and passions, and provide them with the resources and support they need to succeed.

Albert Einstein said, "Everybody is a genius. But if you judge a fish by its ability to climb a tree, it will live its whole life believing that it is stupid." This quote emphasizes the importance of recognizing and nurturing each individual's unique talents and skills.

Maya Angelou, a famous writer, once said, "I've learned that people will forget what you said, people will forget what you did, but people will never forget how you made them feel." This quote emphasizes the importance of creating an environment that fosters positive emotions and encourages people to thrive.

By creating an environment that recognizes and nurtures individual talents, we can help our children reach their full potential and achieve their goals. And by developing self-awareness and setting goals for ourselves, we can lead fulfilling and satisfying lives.

Chapter 9

AWAKENING THE
LIGHT WITHIN

As parents, we play a vital role in shaping the lives of our children. To guide them on their journey toward a fulfilling and purposeful life, it is essential for us to cultivate self-awareness within ourselves. In this chapter, we will explore the importance of self-awareness in conscious parenting and how it lays the foundation for creating a nurturing and empowering environment for our children's growth and development.

SECTION 1: EMBRACING SELF-AWARENESS AS PARENTS

Let us embark on a journey of self-discovery. By cultivating self-awareness, we gain a deeper understanding of our own thoughts, emotions, and behaviors. This self-awareness enables us to model positive attitudes and behaviors for our children as they learn best through our actions. Self-awareness refers to the ability of an individual to recognize and understand their own thoughts, feelings, and behaviors as well as to have an understanding of their own existence as a separate entity from others. Here's an example of self-awareness:

Let's say there is a person named John who is reflecting on his behavior during a recent argument with a close friend. John realizes that he was overly defensive and interrupted his friends while they were expressing their thoughts and feelings. He also noticed that he was feeling insecure and reacted emotionally rather than really listening and trying to understand his friend's perspective. In this moment of reflection, John demonstrates self-awareness by recognizing and acknowledging his own thoughts, emotions, and behaviors.

Based on this self-awareness, John can take further steps to improve. He might apologize to his friend, acknowledge his mistake, and work on active listening skills to better understand others. By recognizing his own actions and emotions, John shows a level of self-awareness that allows him to make positive changes and foster healthier relationships in the future.

PRACTICING SELF-REFLECTION

Take moments of quiet reflection. Reflect on your own values, beliefs, and desires. Explore your strengths and areas for growth. This introspection allows us to align our parenting approach with our true selves, fostering an environment that promotes authenticity and personal growth for both us and our children. Once I had a disagreement with a close friend, and it left me feeling upset and frustrated. After taking some time to process my emotions, I decided to engage in self-reflection to gain a deeper understanding of the situation and my own role in it.

During my self-reflection, I asked myself a series of questions to explore my thoughts, feelings, and actions. I focused on being honest and open with myself, seeking to uncover any biases, assumptions, or patterns that might have influenced the disagreement.

First, I examined my own emotions and reactions during the conflict. I realized that I had become defensive and dismissive of my friend's perspective, which hindered effective communication. I acknowledged that my ego was getting in the way, preventing me from truly listening and empathizing.

Next I considered the underlying factors that contributed to the disagreement. I realized that both my friend and I had different expectations and needs in the situation, but I had failed to recognize or address them. I recognized that my lack of empathy and failure to consider alternative viewpoints had escalated the disagreement.

Additionally, I reflected on my own communication style. I realized that I tend to be assertive and direct in expressing my thoughts, which can sometimes come across as confrontational or dismissive. I acknowledged that my approach might have further fueled the conflict instead of promoting understanding.

I recognized that my personal insecurities and fear of being misunderstood had influenced my behavior. I discovered that I had a tendency to become defensive when my ideas were challenged, which hindered productive dialogue.

Through this process, I realized the importance of active listening and open-mindedness in resolving conflicts. I understood that self-reflection is a crucial tool for personal growth and that it requires humility and a willingness to acknowledge one's own shortcomings.

Armed with these insights, I decided to reach out to my friend to apologize and engage in a genuine conversation. I expressed my understanding of my own role in the disagreement and my commitment to improving our communication. I shared my reflections and asked for their perspective, aiming to rebuild trust and find a common ground.

This example illustrates how self-reflection involves examining one's own thoughts, emotions, and actions to gain insight and understanding. It allows for personal growth, improved relationships, and the development of effective communication skills.

SECTION 2: THE ROLE OF SELF-AWARENESS IN CONSCIOUS PARENTING

PARENTING WITH INTENTION

Conscious parenting begins with setting intentions. By clarifying our values and goals, we can be more intentional in our parenting choices. Self-awareness helps us identify our parenting triggers, biases, and unconscious patterns, enabling us to respond to our children with compassion and understanding.

It's important to acknowledge that parenting can be challenging and exhausting at times. In the face of nagging, tantrums, or negative behavior, it can be tempting for parents to give in and say yes just to put an end to the frustration and exhaustion. However, it is crucial to recognize the potential negative consequences of this approach. When parents give in to their child's demands or negative behavior simply because they are tired and want to avoid further aggravation, it sends a confusing message. Children may interpret this as a sign that persistence pays off and that they can manipulate their parents' decisions through tantrums or repetitive nagging. This can lead to a cycle of problematic behavior and make it even more challenging for parents to establish boundaries and set limits in the future. Moreover, by giving in to their child's demands without proper consideration, parents miss an opportunity to teach important life lessons, such as delayed gratification, resilience, and problem-solving skills. Children need consistent guidance and boundaries to develop a sense of discipline and responsibility. When parents give up easily, it deprives children of valuable opportunities for growth and development.

Parenting requires intentionality and the ability to set aside momentary frustrations in favor of long-term goals and values. While it may be difficult in the moment, finding the strength to stick to your decisions and follow through on established boundaries can be more beneficial for both you and your child in the long run.

I'd like to share an example of parenting with intention. One day, while making plans to meet my friends with my kids at the mall, my two-year-old daughter started having a tantrum. I calmly told her that if she didn't stop, we would turn around and go home. My friends expressed doubt, assuming I wouldn't actually follow through since we had lunch reservations. However, I decided to stay true to my word and we went home. Since that incident, my daughter has learned that when I say something, I mean it. Following through on my words has helped her understand the importance of taking actions and being responsible for her behavior. It has also shown her that there are consequences for our actions. In this case, she experienced firsthand that throwing a tantrum affected our plans for the day.

By following through on what I said I would do, I have built trust with my daughter. She now knows that when I set a boundary or make a statement, I am genuine and consistent. This consistency has helped her feel secure and confident in our relationship.

Parenting with intention and following through on commitments also instills important values in our children. Through this experience, my daughter is learning about accountability, honesty, and integrity. She is understanding that actions speak louder than words and that our words have meaning and power. By modeling these behaviors, I am shaping her character and encouraging her to be authentic in her own actions.

By setting clear expectations, following through on our word, and teaching valuable life lessons, we are helping our children develop into responsible and authentic individuals.

CREATING EMOTIONAL RESONANCE

Let us be attuned to our own emotions. Emotions serve as valuable messengers, guiding us toward our needs and desires. By developing self-awareness of our emotions, we can create an emotional resonance with our children. This resonance fosters a safe space for them to express their emotions and learn healthy ways of navigating their own feelings. Creating emotional resonance is about connecting with others on a human-to-human level, even with our own children. It's important to recognize that as parents, we may not always understand everything our kids are going through, and that's OK. What matters is that we approach conversations with an open mind and a willingness to listen, acknowledging that our children have their own unique perspectives and emotions.

When talking to our kids, it's important to pay attention to how we feel in the moment and allow those emotions to guide us. If we're feeling overwhelmed or frustrated, it's OK to take a step back and take a deep breath. By acknowledging our own emotions, we can approach the conversation with a calmer and more empathetic mindset.

In these moments, we can engage with our children by sharing our own experiences or struggles, even if they may not directly relate to their situation. By opening up and being vulnerable, we create a space for our kids to feel comfortable expressing their own emotions and experiences. This humanizes the conversation and reinforces the idea that we're all navigating life together, learning and growing along the way.

During these conversations, active listening becomes paramount. Truly hearing our children's thoughts and feelings without judgment allows us to understand them better and validate their emotions. Even if we don't fully grasp their perspective, showing empathy and support can help them feel heard and valued.

By talking to our kids as human beings, acknowledging our own limitations, and paying attention to our emotions, we create a foundation of trust and openness. We foster emotional resonance by approaching conversations with empathy and understanding, allowing our children to express themselves authentically. Through these meaningful connections, we build stronger relationships and provide our children with the support they need to navigate life's challenges.

Modeling Self-Acceptance and Growth

As parents, we are our children's first role models. By embracing our own imperfections and demonstrating self-acceptance, we teach our children the importance of self-love and resilience. Our self-awareness allows us to model growth mindset, showing our children that learning and personal development are lifelong journeys.

Section 3: Nurturing Self-Awareness in Children

Encouraging Self-Exploration

Create an environment that encourages self-exploration. Provide opportunities for our children to discover their interests, passions, and talents. Allow them to make choices and express their unique selves. By nurturing their self-awareness, we empower them to make conscious decisions that align with their authentic selves.

Encouraging self-exploration involves creating a space where your child can freely express themselves without judgment and allowing them to discover their own unique interests and talents. It's important for parents to avoid imposing their own style or expectations onto their child's exploration. Instead, the focus should be on nurturing their creativity and guiding them in a supportive manner.

For example, let's say your child shows an interest in painting. Rather than dictating what they should create or how it should look, you provide them with a variety of art materials and let them explore their own ideas. You refrain from criticizing or telling them that their approach is wrong. Instead, you offer gentle guidance and encouragement, inspiring them to experiment and learn new techniques.

If you notice your child struggling with a certain aspect of their painting, you can share your own experiences or demonstrate alternative methods without devaluing their efforts. For instance, you might say, "I love how you used those colors! Have you ever tried blending them together to create a different effect? Let me show you." By offering suggestions in a positive and empowering manner, you provide your child with an opportunity to expand their skills without feeling discouraged or judged.

Throughout the process, you celebrate and appreciate their unique style and choices. You express genuine interest in their creations, asking open-ended questions about their inspiration and what they enjoyed most about their artwork. By valuing their individual expression, you encourage them to trust their instincts and embrace their own artistic voice.

By allowing your child to explore and express themselves without judgment, you create an environment where they feel safe and empowered to discover their own talents and preferences. This approach promotes self-confidence, autonomy, and a love for creative expression. It also teaches them to appreciate the journey of self-discovery and the joy of learning rather than solely focusing on achieving a specific outcome.

Remember as a parent your role is to guide and support your child's self-exploration, allowing them to flourish in their own unique way. By providing a nurturing and nonjudgmental environment, you foster their self-esteem and encourage a lifelong love for self-expression and personal growth.

CULTIVATING MINDFULNESS
AND REFLECTION

Introduce mindfulness practices to our children. Teach them the art of being present and attuned to their own thoughts and emotions. Encourage journaling or reflective exercises to foster self-reflection.

These practices nurture their self-awareness, enabling them to make conscious choices and understand the impact of their actions. Through authentic communication, support, and a nurturing environment, we empower our children to explore their talents and fulfill their true potential.

Cultivating mindfulness and reflection in both us and our children can bring about numerous benefits, such as increased self-awareness, emotional regulation, and overall wellbeing. Here's an example of how you can incorporate mindfulness and reflection into your family's routine:

Let's say that after a busy day, you and your child sit down together before bedtime. You create a calm and quiet space that is free from distractions. You begin by inviting your child to take a few deep breaths, guiding them to focus on the sensation of their breath entering and leaving their body.

After a few moments of quiet breathing, you introduce a reflective question or prompt for your child to ponder. For instance, you might ask, "What is something that made you feel grateful today?" or "Can you think of a moment when you felt proud of yourself?"

You give your child time to reflect and encourage them to share their thoughts. As they express themselves, you actively listen without interrupting or judging their responses. It's important to create a nonjudgmental space where they feel safe to share openly.

After your child has shared their reflections, you can share your own thoughts as well. This allows for a reciprocal exchange, fostering a sense of connection and mutual understanding.

To conclude the mindfulness and reflection session, you can guide your child through a brief gratitude practice. Together, you each mention one or two things you are grateful for from the day. This helps cultivate a positive mindset and encourages appreciation for the small joys in life.

By incorporating these mindful moments into your family's routine, you create an opportunity for self-reflection and introspection. Over time, this practice helps your child develop emotional intelligence, resilience, and a deeper understanding of their own thoughts and feelings.

Remember mindfulness and reflection are ongoing practices. By consistently incorporating these moments into your family's routine, you provide your child with valuable tools to navigate their emotions and develop a greater sense of self-awareness.

Chapter 10

THE WORLD OF SOCIAL MEDIA

RECLAIMING AUTHENTICITY AND DISCOVERING MEANING BEYOND EXTERNAL VALIDATION

In today's digital age, many individuals find themselves seeking validation and defining their self-worth through social media. The allure of curated profiles and the pursuit of likes and followers often leads people to lose touch with their authentic selves. This chapter explores the consequences of such behavior and emphasizes the importance of self-awareness in understanding one's true desires and finding genuine happiness. Furthermore, it addresses the role of parents in guiding their children through the pitfalls of social media and helping them develop healthy boundaries.

THE SUPERFICIALITY OF SOCIAL MEDIA

Social media platforms have become a double-edged sword in modern society. On one side, they provide means of self-expression and connection with others. On the other side, they can easily become a breeding ground for insecurity and comparison. People often strive to present an idealized version of themselves by posting carefully curated photos and seeking validation in the form of likes and comments. However, this pursuit of external affirmation comes at a cost. While spending endless hours trying to perfect the post, to edit the photo and create a story with a message of an amazing life, your children would lack the experience of living in the moment that they are trying to capture. The validation derived from social media can become addictive. The incessant need for likes and positive feedback can gradually erode one's self-esteem, creating a cycle of seeking external approval. When individuals rely heavily on the validation of others to feel good about themselves, their sense of self-worth becomes fragile and unstable. They may lose touch with their own internal compass and become disconnected from their true desires. As soon as they step away from the computer or put down their phone, surroundings become dull and disconnected. The drive to create an alternate reality becomes dominant and takes away from living in the now.

Constantly seeking validation through social media can lead to a disconnection from reality. When life revolves around capturing the perfect photo or presenting a desirable image, genuine experiences and authentic emotions can be overshadowed. The inability to have a genuine conversation or express genuine emotions without posing for a camera becomes a significant concern. I would like to highlight the importance of reconnecting with the present moment and embracing authenticity beyond the confines of social media.

Amid the busyness and distractions of modern life, self-awareness becomes crucial. Taking the time to pause and reflect allows individuals to understand their own feelings, desires, and aspirations. By asking important questions, such as "Who am I?" and "What am I trying to accomplish?" individuals can uncover their true motivations and goals. This introspection enables them to align their actions with their authentic selves rather than being influenced by external opinions and societal pressures.

THE ROLE OF PARENTS

Parents play a vital role in helping their children navigate the challenges of social media and develop healthy boundaries. By being involved in their kids' lives and understanding the impact of social media, parents can guide their children toward self-awareness and authentic self-expression. Furthermore, it is crucial to remember that children often learn more from the observation of their parents' behavior than from their words. When parents prioritize the image of what they post on social media over being present in the current moment, they inadvertently teach their child that online appearances are more important than real-life experiences. This can lead to a loss of connection between parent and child, as the latter observe that social media posts are valued over genuine, in-the-moment interactions. To create healthy relationships and model appropriate social media use, we should strive to be fully present with our children, demonstrating that real-life connections and experiences are far more valuable than any online persona.

KNOWING WHAT'S HAPPENING IN KIDS' LIVES

It is essential for parents to stay informed about their children's online activities and social media usage. By regularly engaging in open and nonjudgmental conversations, parents can create a safe space for their children to share their experiences, concerns, and aspirations. This knowledge allows us to identify any potential negative influences or unhealthy patterns and address them proactively.

Chapter 11

CULTIVATING BALANCE AND RESPECTING PERSONAL LIMITS

You should educate your children about the importance of setting boundaries in the digital world as well as personal interaction. You can discuss the potential pitfalls of seeking validation through social media and help your children develop a healthy perspective. By teaching critical thinking skills and encouraging self-reflection, parents empower children to make informed decisions about their online presence and interactions. Teaching boundaries to children when it comes to the use of social media and interpersonal communication is an important aspect of their overall development and safety. Here are some guidelines to consider:

1. Start early. Introduce the concept of boundaries and consent from an early age. Teach children about personal space and the importance of respecting others' boundaries.
2. Lead by example. Children learn by observing their parents and caregivers. Model healthy boundaries in your own interactions with others, both online and offline. Show them what respectful communication looks like.

3. Open communication. Create an open and nonjudgmental environment where children feel comfortable discussing their experiences and concerns. Encourage them to ask questions and express their opinions.
4. Explain the risks. Discuss the potential risks and consequences associated with the use of social media and other online platforms. Talk about privacy, cyberbullying, and the permanence of online content. Help them understand that their actions online can have real-life implications.
5. Set clear rules and expectations. Establish clear rules and guidelines regarding the use of technology and social media. Discuss appropriate online behavior, time limits, and the importance of seeking permission before sharing personal information or photos.
6. Teach critical thinking. Help children develop critical thinking skills to evaluate online content and interactions. Teach them to question the credibility of information and to think critically before sharing or responding to messages.
7. Encourage empathy. Foster empathy and respect for others' feelings and boundaries. Teach children to consider the impact of their words and actions on others, both online and offline.
8. Establish privacy settings. Show children how to set privacy settings on social media platforms to control who can view their content and interact with them. Explain the importance of keeping personal information private.
9. Monitor and supervise. Regularly monitor your child's online activities and be aware of the platforms they use. Consider using parental control tools or software to help ensure their safety.
10. Encourage breaks and offline activities. Help children find a healthy balance between online and offline activities. Encourage them to engage in hobbies, sports, and face-to-face interactions with friends and family.

Remember that teaching boundaries is an ongoing process, and it's important to adapt to your child's age and maturity level. Stay engaged, have open conversations, and support them in navigating the digital world responsibly.

SETTING POSITIVE EXAMPLES

Parents should be mindful of their own social media behavior and serve as positive examples for their children. By practicing healthy digital habits and demonstrating the value of real-life experiences and connections, parents can inspire their children to prioritize authenticity over external validation. Parental involvement in offline activities, hobbies, and quality family time fosters a sense of fulfillment beyond the virtual world.

One important way to teach your child about boundaries and responsible social media use is by setting a positive example. Start by demonstrating respectful communication in your own online interactions. Show them how to engage in healthy discussions, avoid cyberbullying, and resolve conflicts peacefully. Protect your privacy online by adjusting privacy settings, being cautious about sharing personal information, and explaining the importance of these actions to your child's safety. Mindful sharing is another aspect to focus on. Before posting content, discuss potential consequences and encourage them to consider how it might be perceived by others. Model responsible sharing by only posting appropriate and positive content that adds value to the online community. Additionally, make sure to take regular breaks from technology and engage in offline activities. Spend quality time together, emphasizing the importance of balancing screen time with real-life experiences. When encountering disagreements or negative comments online, demonstrate how to respond with grace and constructive criticism. Show your child the value of empathy and compassion by exhibiting kindness, support, and understanding toward others. Encourage them to consider others' feelings and experiences when engaging with them online. By consistently modeling these positive behaviors, you can help your child develop a strong understanding of boundaries, respectful communication, and responsible online behavior.

Always remember your actions speak louder than words, so leading by example is crucial in teaching them how to navigate the digital world safely and responsibly.

ACTION PLAN

1. *Engage in meaningful conversations.* Set aside regular time to have open and nonjudgmental conversations with your children. Create a safe space where they feel comfortable sharing their thoughts, experiences, and concerns related to social media. Encourage them to reflect on their online interactions, their emotions, and the impact of social media on their self-esteem and overall wellbeing.

   For example, during family meals or dedicated "tech-free" evenings, initiate discussions about social media, its influence, and the importance of self-awareness. Share your own experiences and challenges, fostering an environment of understanding and mutual support.

2. *Explore nature and outdoor activities.* Encourage your children to spend time outdoors and connect with nature. Nature provides a calming and grounding influence, allowing them to step away from the digital world and engage with the real world. Participate in outdoor activities together, such as hiking, gardening, or picnics in the park.

   For example, plan a weekend hike or a family camping trip where everyone can disconnect from technology and immerse themselves in the beauty of nature. Use this opportunity to talk about the benefits of being present in the moment and the importance of finding joy in simple experiences.

3. *Implement tech-free time.* Set specific periods of the day or week where technology is off-limits for everyone in the family. This dedicated tech-free time encourages individuals to engage in activities that promote self-awareness, creativity, and genuine connections.

   For example, designate a certain time each day where all family members put their devices away and engage in activities, such as reading, playing board games, or practicing mindfulness exercises together. Use this time to foster deeper connections and encourage self-reflection.

4. *Foster offline hobbies and pursuits.* Encourage your children to explore hobbies and interests that do not revolve around social media. Engaging in activities that require focus, creativity, and personal growth can help them develop a stronger sense of self and discover what truly brings them joy and fulfillment.

   For example, encourage your child to join a sports team, enroll in art classes, or explore musical instruments. By supporting their offline interests, you provide them with opportunities for self-expression and personal growth outside the realm of social media.

5. *Lead by example.* As a parent, be conscious of your own social media habits and the example you set for your children. Use social media responsibly, emphasizing the value of authenticity and genuine connections. Demonstrate

the importance of balance by prioritizing offline experiences and meaningful interactions.

For example, instead of mindlessly scrolling through social media, engage in activities that align with your values and passions. Share your experiences with your children, showing them that a fulfilling life extends beyond the digital realm.

By implementing this action plan, you can guide your children toward self-awareness and help them understand the importance of finding genuine happiness beyond social media. Through meaningful conversations, nature exploration, tech-free time, offline hobbies, and setting positive examples, you can empower your child to develop healthy boundaries and lead fulfilling lives, both online and offline. It is essential to emphasize the importance of perseverance, especially during the times when things get hard. Let them know it's okay to struggle and face challenges, teaching them not to abandon their efforts when faced with difficulties helps them grow and figure out how to create solutions thorough challenging times in their life. In the end, what they learn from the whole experience is what matters most.

Chapter 12

THE SACRED DANCE OF TRUST

In the sacred dance of trust and open communication, respecting your child's privacy is paramount. Invading their personal space, such as reading their journal without permission, can shatter the foundation of trust that you've diligently built. Instead, cultivating an environment of openness and understanding empowers your child to willingly share their life with you, fostering a strong and authentic parent-child connection.

Consider a situation where you stumble upon your child's journal left unattended. Temptation may arise to delve into its contents, driven by curiosity or concern. However, in that moment, pause and remind yourself of the trust you've nurtured with your child. Respect their privacy and recognize that their journal is a sacred space for self-expression and introspection.

Instead, seize this opportunity to cultivate open communication. Create an atmosphere where your child feels safe to share their thoughts and emotions without fear of judgment or invasion. Initiate heartfelt conversations, expressing your genuine interest in their wellbeing and experiences. Listen actively and empathetically, allowing them to express themselves openly.

For example, suppose your child seems distant or preoccupied. Instead of prying into their journal, engage in a conversation over a cup of tea or during a peaceful walk in nature. Ask gentle and nonintrusive questions about their day or their feelings, allowing them to share at their own pace. Encourage them to speak honestly, assuring them that their thoughts and emotions are valid and valued.

In moments of vulnerability, validate their feelings and reassure them that you are there to support them unconditionally. Avoid rushing to solve their problems; instead, let them know that you believe in their ability to find their own solutions. This empowerment instills confidence in their decision-making and encourages them to turn to you when they need guidance.

As your child opens up, refrain from judgment or criticism, even if their thoughts or experiences differ from your own. Cultivate a deep sense of acceptance and understanding, emphasizing that you are there to listen and support, regardless of the circumstances.

By creating open communication and mutual trust, your child will be more likely to share their thoughts, dreams, and challenges willingly. A strong sense of trust will develop, enriching your parent-child relationship and nurturing their emotional wellbeing.

Open communication is a two-way street. Be open to sharing your own experiences and emotions with your child, allowing a sense of vulnerability and connection. By sharing stories from your own life, you demonstrate that you, too, are human, with strengths and vulnerabilities, and that it is safe for them to do the same.

In the dance of trust and open communication, the parent-child bond blossoms into a harmonious symphony of understanding and love. Respecting your child's privacy while encouraging open sharing creates an atmosphere where trust thrives and your child feels empowered to navigate life's journey with the loving guidance and support you provide. Together, you cocreate a sanctuary of trust and understanding, deepening the sacred connection that transcends time and space.

Chapter 13

INNER RADIANCE

Raising confident kids requires a thoughtful and nurturing approach. Here are some key strategies, along with examples of what to do and what to avoid, to help foster confidence in children:

First and foremost, it's essential to provide unconditional love and support. Show your children that you love and accept them for who they are, regardless of their achievements or mistakes. For example, when your child receives a lower grade on a test, avoid saying things like "You're stupid." Instead, reassure them that everyone makes mistakes, and emphasize that their worth is not determined by their academic performance.

Encouraging independence and decision-making is crucial for building confidence. Allow your children to make age-appropriate choices and decisions. For instance, let them choose their extracurricular activities or decide what clothes to wear (within reasonable limits). This empowers them and helps develop their problem-solving skills. By trusting them to make decisions, you show that you have confidence in their abilities.

In addition to celebrating achievements, praise your child's effort and progress. Rather than solely focusing on grades or awards, acknowledge their hard work and improvements. For example, instead of saying, "You're so smart," say, "I'm proud of how you studied diligently for the test and improved your understanding of the subject." This teaches them that effort and dedication are important qualities and boosts their confidence in their abilities.

Teach resilience and positive thinking to help children develop a strong sense of self-confidence. When they face challenges or setbacks, guide them in finding solutions and encourage a positive mindset. For example, if they don't make the sports team they wanted, remind them that they can learn from the experience and improve their skills for the next opportunity. This instills confidence in their ability to overcome obstacles and bounce back from disappointments.

Creating a supportive and positive environment is crucial for nurturing confidence. Foster open communication, and provide a space where your child feels safe to express themselves without fear of judgment. Actively listen to their thoughts and ideas. For example, when they share their interests or passions, show genuine interest and ask questions to encourage further exploration. This validates their self-worth and boosts their confidence.

Avoid excessive criticism and negativity. Be mindful of your words and refrain from constant criticism or negative comments. Instead, provide constructive feedback and guide your children toward improvement. For instance, instead of saying, "You always make mistakes," say, "Let's work together to find a solution." This helps them develop a growth mindset and maintain confidence in their abilities.

Set realistic expectations for your children. Help them establish attainable goals and expectations. This enables them to experience success and build confidence as they achieve their objectives. For example, if your child is learning to ride a bike, set small milestones and celebrate their progress along the way. This boosts their confidence and motivates them to keep trying.

Be a positive role model. Children often learn by observing their parents. Model self-confidence and positive self-talk in your own life. For instance, if you make a mistake, demonstrate how to learn from it and move forward with resilience. This greatly influences their perception of themselves and encourages them to adopt a confident mindset.

Encourage self-care and self-expression. Teach your children the importance of taking care of their physical and emotional wellbeing. Encourage them to express their feelings and opinions, fostering a sense of self-awareness and confidence. For example, provide opportunities for them to engage in activities they enjoy, such as drawing, dancing, or writing, which allows them to express themselves and boosts their confidence.

Building confidence takes time and consistency. By implementing these strategies, such as providing unconditional love, encouraging independence, and fostering a positive environment, you can help your children develop a strong sense of self-worth and confidence as they navigate through life.

Chapter 14

PARENTING STYLE SELF-REFLECTION TEST

Understanding our parenting style is a crucial step toward conscious and mindful parenting. This self-reflection test aims to help you explore your parenting approach, identify areas of strength, and uncover opportunities for growth. Embrace this exercise as a pathway to becoming a more intentional and conscious parent.

Instructions: Answer the following questions honestly by selecting the option that best describes your usual response or behavior in each scenario. After completing the test, review your answers and reflect on the provided examples for conscious parenting implementation.

SELF-REFLECTION TEST

1. When your child makes a mistake, how do you typically respond?
   a) Get upset and criticize their actions.
   b) Punish them without discussing the situation.

c) Use it as a learning opportunity and discuss their actions with empathy and understanding.

2. How often do you engage in active listening when your child expresses their thoughts or feelings?
   a) Rarely. I tend to dismiss their emotions.
   b) Sometimes. But I often get distracted.
   c) Regularly. I make an effort to listen attentively and validate their feelings.

3. How do you handle conflicts between siblings?
   a) Ignore the situation and hope it resolves on its own.
   b) Intervene but take sides, without understanding both perspectives.
   c) Facilitate a calm and respectful discussion to address the root of the issue.

4. When your child accomplishes something significant, how do you react?
   a) Brush it off or don't pay much attention to it.
   b) Offer praise without acknowledging their effort.
   c) Celebrate their achievement and acknowledge their hard work and dedication.

5. How do you approach discipline and setting boundaries?
   a) Use strict rules without explaining the reasons behind them.
   b) Set rules but rarely follow through with consequences.
   c) Establish clear boundaries with explanations and age-appropriate consequences.

6. How often do you make time for self-care and personal growth?
   a) Rarely. I feel guilty taking time for myself.

b) Sometimes. But it's sporadic and inconsistent.

c) Regularly. I prioritize self-care to be a more present and patient parent.

7. How do you encourage your child's interests and passions?
   a) Dismiss their interests if they don't align with my own.
   b) Show mild interest but don't actively support their pursuits.
   c) Support and encourage their interests, providing opportunities for exploration.

8. How do you handle disagreements or arguments with your child?
   a) Assert your authority and expect obedience without discussion.
   b) Give in to avoid conflicts, even if you disagree with them.
   c) Engage in open dialogue, respecting their viewpoint and finding compromises.

RESULTS AND CONSCIOUS PARENTING EXAMPLES

- Mostly A's: Your parenting style might lean toward an authoritarian approach. Implement conscious parenting by taking time to understand your child's emotions and perspectives, encouraging open communication, and fostering a supportive environment for growth.

- Mostly B's: Your parenting style may display elements of a permissive approach. Embrace conscious parenting by setting clear boundaries with consistent consequences, actively listening to your child, and being more involved in their interests and pursuits.

- Mostly C's: Congratulations! Your responses indicate a more conscious and mindful parenting style. Continue nurturing open communication, active listening, and empathy to further enhance your parent-child connection.

Self-reflection is a powerful tool in becoming a more conscious parent. By identifying areas for growth and implementing conscious parenting practices, you create a nurturing and supportive environment for your child's development and overall wellbeing. Embrace this journey of self-awareness and mindful parenting to create a deep and loving relationship with your child.

Chapter 15

THE HEART-CENTERED PATH OF CONSCIOUS PARENTING

My belief regarding humanity is that we are here to truly experience life, and the purpose of our existence is to find happiness. I firmly believe that if we live from the heart and cultivate gratitude, life will be filled with pure joy. Fear, in this context, can be seen as an acronym for "false evidence appearing real." It is a deceptive emotion that often holds us back and prevents us from moving forward in life. Fear has the ability to paralyze us, hindering our progress and potential. However, by understanding our emotions and being mindful of our feelings, we can easily identify fear for what it truly is and learn to overcome it. Once we grasp this understanding, we can break free from the limitations of fear and take positive steps toward personal growth and fulfillment.

In addition, I believe it is crucial to guide our children toward a life of abundance and harmony. By helping them comprehend their emotions, fostering self-awareness, and teaching them the power of gratitude, we empower them to navigate life's challenges with resilience and a positive mindset. By instilling in them a belief in abundance and harmony, we equip them with the necessary tools to create fulfilling and joyful lives for themselves and others.

I firmly hold the belief that by embracing love, gratitude, and self-awareness, while simultaneously conquering fear, we can truly experience the fullness of life and set the stage for future generations to live lives abundant in happiness and harmony.

CONCLUSION

In conclusion, I would like to express my deepest gratitude for joining me on this transformative journey of conscious parenting. Throughout these pages, we have explored the principles, practices, and insights that can help us become more aware, present, and intentional in our roles as parents.

My greatest hope is that this book has inspired you to cultivate a deeper connection with yourself, your children, and the world around you. My intent is that it has empowered you to embrace the joys and challenges of parenting with a newfound sense of purpose and mindfulness.

As you continue on your own unique path of conscious parenting, remember to be gentle with yourself. Parenting is not about achieving perfection but about showing up with love, authenticity, and a willingness to learn and grow alongside your children. Cherish the beautiful moments, learn from the difficult ones, and always hold space for open communication and understanding.

May your journey be filled with moments of laughter, love, and deep connections with your children. May you embrace the power of your influence and recognize the immense impact you have on shaping the lives of your little ones. And above all, may you find fulfillment, joy, and abundance in the incredible journey of parenting.

May this book serve as a reminder that we hold the power to shape the future through our conscious choices. Let us embark on this journey of love and gratitude with renewed conviction and determination. May we lead our children by example, inspiring them to be compassionate, empathetic, and courageous individuals.

I am grateful for the opportunity to share these insights with you, and I believe that as we embrace love, gratitude, and self-awareness, we unlock the true essence of life. Together, let us set the stage for a world abundant in happiness and harmony where parenting becomes a guiding light for generations to come.

Thank you for joining me on this extraordinary voyage to practicing mindful parenting while fostering the growth of children's talents and providing an environment for them to flourish. Thank you for allowing me to be a part of your parenting experience. I wish you and your family an abundance of love, happiness, and meaningful connections as you continue to navigate the beautiful adventure of conscious parenting.

Printed in the United States
by Baker & Taylor Publisher Services